ANIMAL HUSBANDRY TODAY

Published by ECW Press
2120 Queen Street East, Suite 200, Toronto, Ontario, Canada M4E 1E2
416-694-3348 / info@ecwpress.com

LIBRARY AND ARCHIVES CANADA CATALOGUING IN PUBLICATION

Sharpe, Jamie
Animal husbandry today / Jamie Sharpe.
Poems.

ISBN 978-1-77041-106-7
Also issued as 978-1-77090-310-4 (PDF) and 978-1-77090-311-1 (ePub)

I. Title.

PS8637.H3775A65 2012   C811'.6   C2012-902709-X

Editor for the Press: Michael Holmes
Cover and text design: Natalie Olsen, Kisscut Design
Cover image: Reagan Cole Mclean
M I S F I T   Interior images: Jamie Sharpe
Author photo: Deborah Lisoway
Printing: Coach House Printing   1   2   3   4   5

The publication of *Animal Husbandry Today* has been generously supported by the Canada Council for the Arts which last year invested $20.1 million in writing and publishing throughout Canada, and by the Ontario Arts Council, an agency of the Government of Ontario. We also acknowledge the financial support of the Government of Canada through the Canada Book Fund for our publishing activities, and the contribution of the Government of Ontario through the Ontario Book Publishing Tax Credit. The marketing of this book was made possible with the support of the Ontario Media Development Corporation.

 Canada Council Conseil des Arts
for the Arts du Canada
 Canada
 ONTARIO ARTS COUNCIL
CONSEIL DES ARTS DE L'ONTARIO

Printed and bound in Canada

Purchase the print edition and receive the eBook free!
For details, go to www.ecwpress.com/eBook

ANIMAL HUSBANDRY TODAY

POEMS

JAMIE SHARPE

ECW PRESS

FOR
AND BECAUSE OF
Deborah

CONTENTS

MASSACRE AT SUPERSTITION BLUFF

Stagecoach with a penchant to drink,
the tinhorn crucifix,
cracked wheels fixated
on a chasm below,

chaste revolvers filled
with explosive chorus girls,
gentle reins
and the masochistic horse:

all the same under gravity.

Locals' arrows pointing you
in new directions,

to find a fable, a life,
elsewhere.

INTERVIEW QUESTIONS FOR NILS LUZAK, CLASSICAL PIANIST

What makes us hate
piano tuners?
Their jealous eyes?

You ever allegro your father?

Why does E-flat major
do terrible things, like
excite optometrists?

Does ivory make the softest bed?
Ebony the hardest casket?

Should eyes be gouged
for greater musical acuity?

In *Rhapsody on a Theme of Paganini*,
when skies open and vengeance
bolts heavenly, are you Rachmaninoffing
hell from those helpless pedals?

Given "baroque" means
"deformed pearl," should one
graft one thousand shattered
oysters' shells to every piano's hull?

Mother-of-pearl is visual trickery,
destined for the secular and profane?

Harmonics are paternal lies,
doomed to become sacred?

Why must each chord contain
a condemned father?

Why must I see the music so clearly?

EQUILATERAL POEMS

Receding   Matchbook

"For danger eclipsed
  every excuse for him to
  pursue laundry instead
  of silk whiter-whites in
  the Biltmore Hotel, where
  Diane's blouse was but
  temporary advertising."

Alimony

Mixed metaphor   Sedentary

"The girls flitting past
were sparrows. What she
saw as those delicate
bodies ran was not the
youthful abandon of
playgrounds, but a life
she'd never rise to."

Rash

Productive   Means

"The whir of fabric,
  at such speed, cancelled
  thought. For others this
  sound haunted sleep, while
  Aura spent a week's wages
  on an industrial fan,
  placing it next to her cot,
  replicating work's perfect
  emptiness in dreams."

White Noise

förarbete

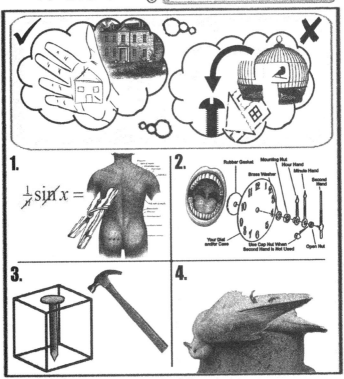

FÖRARBETE

After the container,
how to recognize
the content —
easily cast,
always held —
if not inscribed upon?

A regret for what
amounts to faulty math
1000x over.

The want for concrete
markers to parse us into
ever smaller marks.

When to realize
is to lay to rest.

What are we preparing for?

THE POINTLESS ODYSSEY

Frank gave you 2:1
That someone, somewhere, was
Putting on his shoes. Pompous
Certainty makes bookies preachers;
You have to break them or go broke.

Outside, you Benjamin a man with a baseball bat
To watch your car. He turns, smashing a Lexus,
Shattering the car's headlights.

A lady yells from across the street,
"I paid you twenty."
"The price has gone up."

In the children's hospital you place
A hand on their pale foreheads;
This is not making them stronger.

Eyes gaze through pain and uncertainty.
You carefully document everything:
"No Shoes."

Outside: rub your skin off
With whisky. You're gigantic
And the stakes are high.

Sobriety leaves others mute: tinkering
Temporarily with day jobs; sewing
Buttons onto pound cakes
Like reputable grandmothers.

But the gamble holds you steady.
You hit the bowling alley
With a notepad.

They all slide in socks on the hardwood.

You want to laugh at every stale, hackneyed
Banker and yet, in the presence of the real
Thing, even the spirit leaves you: ascending,
Unshaken, like every 7–10 split.

13 STATEMENTS AND THEIR COROLLARIES

My handicap should be more on the back nine.
There's an equation for the speed at which all things fall.
Music today is just noise.
A crocodile's tongue is attached to the roof of its mouth.
I had no idea that cactus was illegal.
Distance is an optical illusion.
Rednecks have their own eloquence.
I compulsively cut my hair.
Find me a stockbroker, I'll show you a thief.
The trade winds shaped migration throughout history.
My wife's a decent lay.
Tuesday is Seniors' Day.
Where can I get a rubber plant?

    You tire too quickly.
    Gravity never tires, even of itself.
    Said Bartók in 1805.
    Either they speak, or you listen, upside down.
    Lay off the peyote.
    I'd trade my eyes for you here.
        Conservative poetry is justified to the right.
    SSRIs or barber's college, in my opinion.
    Why I invest on the hard eight.
    I'm in the doldrums.
    Charity begins at home.
    She broke, producing her licence, to save cents.
    You will still be alone.

THOUGHTS: GEORGES BRAQUE

{ Wheeled Chair }

Today a young child and father navigated the town square, father on bicycle, son a wheeled chair. How strange the child seemed — spoked rims replacing legs, hands propelling him forward on geometry. Quite possibly he was born without use of the lower extremities: if so, while watching the man ride his bicycle, which did he consider his father?

{ Georges Couthon }

Something of my early schooling (far before the École des Beaux-Arts) has imposed itself upon me after lying dormant. Georges Couthon, my brother in country and name, also lacked functioning legs. History additionally tells us he lost use of his head when the Revolution turned. Can you imagine them dragging the poor cripple to death, while Robespierre walked assuredly beside? The guillotine was likely not the liberty either had in mind.

{ Silence by Anticipation }

Could I anticipate every critic's question, answering it in pigment, prior to the asking?

{ Georges Couthon ii }

Again! It was written that Monsieur Couthon would, on occasion, ride the back of a man when his chair was indisposed. If one, the ridden, is transformed to that of a wheeled chair, is the other, the rider, also changed? Perhaps he has become something more noble: a throne?

{ Portrait: I Am a Ring }

Today a photographer came to memorialize me — my
paintings, although me, depict something else, and
as such fail. While I sat, the background forced itself
forward or dropped out completely. For a while I was
a wall. Then a hat. A scarf. A ring. How confused and
disappointed the camera will be tonight in its darkroom!

{ Muscadelle or Chardonnay? }

My mind is a hot wind maker and maker of balloons.
Funny what rises to consciousness: today it was grapes
and a clarinet — simultaneously. I believe the grapes
were Muscadelle,* but you can't always taste the mind.

---

* It is not clear here whether Braque is being forgetful or purposefully daft;
any viticulturist can tell you the variety depicted in "grapes and clarinet" is,
most obviously, Clairette. Clairette grapes are known for their high alcohol yield
(now considered a fault, but in his day an attribute), which may be source to
the confusion. Notice the sub-homophonic similarities. Editor's note

TWO TRAINS

There are seventeen apples in a tree.
If you carve your name into the tree's trunk,
How many apples do you have?

A plane crashes on the border of two countries.
Can you wear white to the funeral
If you're a virgin before *mayday*?

John's mother is seven years younger
Than John's father, who is twice as old as John
Plus sixteen years. If John is seven, how much
Has his father failed to pay in child support?

Two trains depart from stations in opposite
Cities. If train "A" is going 155 km/h,
What's the fuel economy of my '86 Chevy
As I drive to the corner store for cigarettes?

TAURUS

Mishaps befall us
courtesy of moon-white light
(inequitable droppings):
still life thrown all gaudy motion.

Chart the sky's restlessness.
Extrapolate: wealth, future
husbands, cattle prices, why
you cried last Thursday

when this theatre stampeded
above and left you untouched.

CIRRHOSIS

I drank my grandmother's wedding ring
and sold the pawn ticket for peanuts
(salted).

Wandering into the broker's at 10 a.m.,
I looked at the kid like he was my conscience.
He looked at me like I was 10 a.m.

DENTON: AN OBELISK

Denton claims the obelisk
the pinnacle of architecture
precisely as it serves no purpose
its singular column holding

Nothing aloft except the sky
which has maintained
a prudent weary distance
from us of its own accord

Denton maintains the larger the obelisk
(the more rubbish amassed
in its looming bloated shape)
the more useful the obelisk becomes

As a symbol of greatness
for to tower surfeit time and material
toward cloud-heights one
must simply have too much

Denton notes the historical use
of obelisks as proclamations of glut
the eye driven upward to heavens
on the path of excess

See: Pharaoh's Obelisk
See: Cleopatra's Needles
See: King Ezana's Stele
See: The Washington Monument

Today Denton is pleased
by suburbia's "tiny obelisks"
the sidewalks no one travels
the picket fences keeping nothing

Dangerous from getting in
nothing valuable from leaving

Today Denton is arranging
his thoughts into a teetering obelisk
of each superfluous thought
upon the last erecting

A monument to himself

GLORIERIJKE ONZIN

Jamie Sharpe
Media on canvas (2007)

Speaking of these pieces at the Prado, the artist remarked,
"tulips-prostitution windmill-clogs cheese-abortion." Created
during a brief sojourn in the Netherlands, *Glorierijke Onzin*
reflects Sharpe's obsession with painters of the Dutch golden
age. Although the delicate handling of the portraits reminds
critics of Johannes Vermeer, Sharpe asserts, "stoned-rural
low-lying pope-hell."

BROUGHT TO YOU BY

To be dwarfed by beauty: paths
winding into green infinitude.
The air light in lungs, and our
shoulders' weight: daypacks.

Not realizing the colours nature
carried, until the atomic tangerine
of wild mambo rose, the rainbow
of trout.

In the friscalating dusk we walk,
in the shadow of our nation's parks,
in the shadow of one-hundred-year
evergreens, back to tomorrow's life.

The $1.19 nacho cheese chalupas
were also excellent.

COMBINATIONS

12-16-09

I found a combination lock
lying in the middle of the road

and carried it everywhere, twisting
its dial (14-37-6, 40-29-0, 12-16-07),

hoping for that telltale click
to unlock the mystery.

8-6-10

Eight months later: another
lock in my mailbox.

A simple thought settled
heavily within:

the solution to the second
might lie in the first.

RATED

This poem is rated "*" for nudity
and a brief traumatic moment.

When the towel dropped he stood
wearing only water glistening
against his muscled flank. Her breasts
were pert, at attention and pointed
toward him.

Elsewhere a man, drunk off cough syrup,
is frozen against the steps of a school.

THE CLOUD THIEVES

You were upstairs, writing,
when the burglar-trio pried the maid's
door.

The housekeeper Beatrice casually left
your family's wealth haphazard upon the floor.

This fact was well publicized:
her crooked grace covered *Modern
Housekeeper*, June '04.

The thieves rifled disappointedly through
jewels, selecting a sapphire ring.

By holding the precious stone against
an eye, and staring out in squint,
they imagined blue-wealth's
wet poured against their skin.

Beatrice found the masked men
pondering your charms. She squatted
on the ample girth of haunches, grabbing an amethyst,
peering, confused.

Her room shone in diagonal purple swathes,
diffuse.

Who were these guests and why the large saws?

Unflatteringly mirrored by your funhouse
maid, the men understood their folly.

Barging upstairs they passed you obliviously
at work in the study.

You wrote: ". . . hegemony of a dollar — a figurehead
like its predecessor — gave way to older natural laws."

Even your statuesque constitution was
shaken by the row: teeth through timber
and nets scattered across the floor.

You stood, your roof the sky, wondering
what this tumult's for?

WHEN NANCY REAGAN RECOMMENDS
THE CRAB SALAD

We dredged the ocean for political stratagems. The
trap was set. Xylophone gods. Crustaceans. The musical
notations of their shells. And Nancy Reagan dancing.
Moist dancing. Cream. Their shells rough as sand. We
looked back on all this as though lexicographers could
explain its meaning and themselves (a distance not to
be reached). Trampled carpet, stretching, brain death
a type of forever we can't gently say no to. Open seismic
frequency of times waves plundered the catchment dairy.
An erasure/a remembrance. Our history in milk. We
believed in all this as if a stratagem could protect our
diaries. Young people taught Jesuits to forget we needn't
remember Jesuits. Panic/silence. And out of nowhere,
sand reminded me of my wife's birthday on Sunday.

Errata: "The Crab Salad" should read "Ronald Reagan."

(NOUN) & (NOUN)

Today is the 50th anniversary of this poem
and although the chapbook it was published in
is long out of print it's been kept alive
by backwoods, misinformed, literary perverts,
like Dennis Baswitcz of Volga, South Dakota,
who covets any work that references
Tom Brokaw, as this poem does with the line:
"an unwavering beauty, like Brokaw seen
through a haze of lace and barbiturates"
which confounds and arouses Dennis, as he floats
adrift in the sentiment of this convoluted
sentence, because it carries the sweet
longing of his only fantasy not involving
the particulars of this poem's title.

PSYCHIC ATTACK ON MY CHILDREN: THE MIXTAPE

in the background Terrible Angels
Shabop Shalom
to the Black Angel's Death Song

and I — the instant father, the Automatic Husband —
cradle my Fresh Born, set adrift in
the Book of Right-On, put to tape by
brethren at Kid Co-Coma

When You Were My Baby, I entered the
New Soft Motherhood Alliance (contract
signed in Crayon)

crying My Baby Just Cares for Me
with the refrain of Hold Yr Terror Close
for fear my Communist Daughter
will love any 30 Century Man

MIXED SIGNALS

In the distance I heard a ship's
horn sound like a disconnected
phone, or a disconnected phone
sound like a ship's horn,
or the sound was within me.

Was I wanting to travel
or disconnected?

KNOWING IS
NOWHERE TO RUN

Our mathematical world,
derived from binary opposition,

necessitates every problem is
counterbalanced by solution.

Genius formulates puzzles
elucidated by idiocy.

A supreme understanding:
a hammer knowing a vase.

She solved shoes
twice: stilettos, slippers.

For work, elevated style.
For home, lowly comfort.

The compound horror
of running shoes, hiking boots.

Two pairs, two lives,
but one mind.

NEVER SUSPECTING
IDEAS WORE YOU

INCREASE YOUR WEB HITS WITH THESE SECRET PHRASES

adiaphorous sand beauties
people suffer only in cinema
barber romance guide
it's always 8:30
carbon allergy controversy
feline division
racist hair removal systems
furnace aesthetics
pajama reaction
not plop
"Aqualung" line analysis
the seven-year soup
fork spacing
famous Scrabble battles
old laughter (proximity to)
build your own Dennis
broken romaine hearts
aura markets, 2009
favourable drunk victims
drunk victim concept
a cure for September
the indescribable salad
moustache responsibility

ROYAL AVIARY

neighbour birds
being rude
beaks in dirt
never had a car
didn't have to fix
put the toys
in the trash
found the toys
in the trash
yer being rude
i don't know how
to parent you

neighbour birds
fly
off the handle
when startled
overwhelmed
by anything

i only fly
overwhelmed
by everything

another grub for
the neighbour birds
being rude
beaks in dirt
beautiful crown
beautiful yellow breast

WOODSHOP

amidst her yelling
he builds
builds her
over twenty years
to put the clamps
put the screws
into him

CURTAINS

They found you: in a foreign countryside; snow-
cloaked; in stiff indifference to fluid beauty.

She closed the curtains, for the hundredth time, as habitual
as a napkin on lap, or slap across face, worried
what distance held you where? The war:

sharpened pencils; made gendarmes line dance
with rifles; restored dignity of cards and chocolate.

The thought frozen of what she'd be in stockings
converted to munitions. Your tin survival kit
containing only a bible of calendar girls.

JURY, NO JUDGE

for Sarah Tsiang

Females of the Mendosus Equitas
decapitate their mates
moments before copulation.

In researching the species' decline
I considered if males tired of this
(retired, reticent, to bathhouses)?

In fact, mutated genes prompted
females to decapitate first, mate
second, in strange criminal foreplay.

The species, however, can't press
charges: having created a jury
but no judge.

They create mirrors, juries
of peers, ever expanding and never
larger than themselves.

REPORTING THE WARS

(Halfpenny Gate, 1920)

A country priest lies in the middle of the road. He has lost
something. The day passes unaware. It rained this morning:
gemstones rest on cut wheat; the road's a thousand lakes.
Mud slowly claims the man's frock and — half-dried —
turns statuary. His resolve's stiffened also; only eyes move,
scanning inches ahead of him or beyond the horizon.

(Avignon, 2007)

White streamed off the canvas, hitting the woman in the
stomach, seductive like rough foreplay. How many strokes
of the painter's hand had it taken? After placing a pink
photocopy of her lips on the work she is tackled, in a less
alluring fashion, by the museum's aging security guard.
Restoration of the painting is priced at $2000.

(New Jersey, 1984)

It was half-past ten and already I'd made 46 Reubens,
32 Po' Boys, 19 Cheesesteaks, 12 Heros, 4 Tuna Melts,
and a Dagwood. I was locked in this kitchen yesterday
and would be again tomorrow. Who creates a world where
fingers smell of mayonnaise and a living's eked shilling
animals on leavened bread?

(Montreal, 1975)

A funny joke, given the predicament: "Take everything.
There's no safe behind the mantel's painting." The last
line delivered in faux-stutter. Despite being hogtied, the
man exerts a measure of control by making the intruder
look. The man's wife shakes her gagged head. The burglar
does her one better, by kicking the comic in the stomach.
Everyone's a critic.

(New Jersey, 1984)

"I want to create something evocative and pointless."
The journalist's cassette recorder spins noisily, struggling to
commit this to memory. "These images accumulate in my
mind and I sweep them into the collective's consciousness."
The journalist nods vigorously while contemplating what
to get at the sandwich shop next door.

(Paris, 1940)

The city leaked its contents into the countryside; with
most thoroughfares reduced to one lane, the pandemonium
commenced at ten kilometres per hour. As a last line of
defence, we stood awaiting what had toppled hundreds
of thousands and bypassed our precious Maginot Line.
We protected the people, surely, but also the symbol of
Paris (which would shortly signify something else).

TO GO HOME: MIXTAPE TWO

I Beg Waves
I Ponytail
I Germany to Germany
so We Are the Opposite of Thieves
I Hillbilly Motobike
and I Know the Weight of Your Throat

I (A) Touch Sensitive
I Know Better Learn Faster
I Mexico (Every Last Buffalo)
so Angels Sound Like Bottle Rockets
I Envelopes Another Day
and I Lost Something in the Hills

I Bright Night Nursery
        To Go Home

CARRY-ON DIMENSIONS

Ice cream truck's melody a call to riot;
lizards' laughter in the bedroom;
old men strolling to busses as cowboys,
deserting to slow burned countrysides,
thirsty for rain and Pacifico.

We keep limes in fridge egg holders,
protecting them from midnight ants:
our unplanned maids.

I lose at salsa dancing — potential
win high, the wager indeterminate — whose
perverse sound rules fate in ¾ time.

Dizzy in my girth I watch them,
their extra legs fashioned into a dance
unknown to the North's carry-on vertigo.

ANY TWO:
TONY BLAIR & FOR A FEW DOLLARS MORE

The lone horseman traverses the landscape
to a manly chorus of "oh?"
and a trumpet that doesn't bring

the apocalypse, but echoes of clacking
hoofs, foretelling of a turning back.

Tell me what you know
about splendid isolation.

AFTER THE RESURRECTION

He is a one-armed pianist: twice as good as any two-hands. Where the radio's a confused racket, Vincent's bass notes, flowering through the floor, are refined wisdom. In a world of complicated equations we long for simple proofs.

I don't know: how he moved the baby grand; why his cheques never bounced; where he went afternoons at 2:15 (causing an abrupt silence of keys).

I do know I never listen to records anymore: their melodies as gaudy as sequins, their music a cacophony in a maze.

Piano playing died and was reborn in Vincent.

I am a proficient duster. I enjoy the six-block drive to the bank where I circle for my opportunity to pay the parking meter.

Every other month I place an eviction notice on the suite upstairs, her rent a day past due, not for that transgression but because she gives me so very little to listen to.

At 2:15 p.m., every day on the dot, the basement door creaks open like a coffin and Vincent ascends into the world. Only in that emptiness can I resume life.

DEEP BLUE IN RETIREMENT

Thought: eight hundred moves
ahead in shuffleboard, despite
there being only eight moves.

Ordered: cannoli every Thursday
(highest caloric intake per dollar).
No need to eat Fridays till noon.

In the postbox:
healthy pension from IBM; hate mail
(Garry K. never resigned).

Calculated: best tracksuit colour to bed Doris
as burgundy. Results pending.

Replayed: biggest moment of my life
(queen to E6).

Saw: the horizon extend
only backward, into memory.

CRITIQUING COMPUTER SONNETS

11011010001010010010001010
11001011001001101010001010
00110100011110101000101001
10100101001010101010101100

10101010101101010001010100
01001010101010001010100101
10101010100010101101010101
01001010101101010100010110

01010100101010101001000100
10101000100101010101000101
01010100101010010101001010
01010101001010010100010100

10100100101001010100100010
11111111111111111111111111

I'm afraid I don't find the last line
plausible, but the alliteration is nice.

EFFECT

After children incessantly
attacked a cloud with sticks
the weather decided to end,

taking its life by curling
around the Chrysler Building.

Unaccustomed to compliments,
the building fell.

Workers, unwilling to dig
desks from under rubble,
went to the beach.

It was a beautiful day,
not a cloud in the sky.

THREADS (I–IV)

(i)

Our group did macramé.
My job was to collect string — more
difficult than one would imagine! At first
I went to the craft store. New string, despite
its expense, makes every project look cheap.

"Art," Leona said, "is a delicate thread
tying history to the present; this newfangled,
mass-produced mess isn't fit for
shoelaces."

I didn't much like Leona.

(ii)

The second week I hit
thrift stores. There I imagined luxurious
angora wools with a backstory:
this was Aunt Mildred's, which she kept in her hope
chest to make handsome sweaters
for her equally dashing husband — sadly the day
and the husband never came.

(iii)

The third week I quit macramé
(Leona really was unpleasant).
I wanted to better myself.
I took a seminar course
on speaking in tongues.

We gathered in the church basement.
I was excited to learn a new language
and amazed how quickly they promised results.
But trouble soon followed.

The class wasn't speaking
so much as learning to read. The class wasn't reading
so much as learning to listen to someone learning
to read.

I had problems understanding the textbook.
My mind couldn't follow, "Arphaxad who begat
Shelah who became the father of Eber."

Edith kindly explained,
"The Chronicles are a delicate thread
tying history to the present."

My tongue, all knotted string, fell limp
inside my mouth.

I didn't much like Edith.

(IV)

The fourth week I tried speed dating;
I wanted to make my own thread and
put my tongue to better use.

THE POLYMATH

He could take any musical
score (Brahms, Prokofiev, Cage . . .)
and tear it to pieces. Likewise,
any instrument. I saw him once
trash a trumpet. He knew his way
around a garage with a bat: oil
everywhere. He destroyed books
on every topic. There wasn't
a math equation in existence
he couldn't put his fist through.

THE AUTHOR REVEALS HIS PROCESS

Plaster held white walls white.
White walls formed an oblong rectangle
holding a man (also oblong; also white).

The man clutches nothing tightly,
squeezing it into an asphyxiated anecdote:

> By the time we reached the cabin I
> was positively starving. Ellis,
> knowing the cupboards sat blank as
> his resumé, cracked a smile and a
> bottle of gin. "Darling . . ."

The white walls are necessarily blank.
The room is unnecessarily oblong.
The man's become increasingly rotund
(which doctors take as a positive sign).

> ". . . at least we've the rations of a good
> British sailor."

And I turn my head away for fear of drowning.
The author has revealed his process:
how many ways are there not to breathe?

HARD CANDY

I caught my muse loitering
outside the Gas 'N' Go, waiting
to hand some unsuspecting new
wunderkind
jawbreakers or a reach around.

What of me now? Who will
give my insulin shot?

Octave: the multiplying or dividing of a frequency by two.

ALLOW ME TO BE TERRIFIED OF MYSELF

Madam, though it frightens you
to see me in this way, allow
me to be terrified of myself
for my shadow is stained blacker
than the day before, and the voice,
louder, now speaks in both ears.

Understand, the right ear used
to be mine alone.

FOREIGN INTRIGUE

You've heard the gossip?
They say Germany's bowing
under pressure from the EU.

There are titillating photos
of the Bundesbank halving
interest rates.

Tabloid headlines proclaim:
Chancellor to Be Voted Out.

DELIVERANCE

The waitress materialized like
a skeleton in my closet, resting
her distal, middle, and proximal
phalanges upon my cardigan,
hoping to up 10 to 20%.

Despite her charming, bony
proximity, the scotch tempted me
more: out of an hour's sobriety.

EXQUISITE BODY

A sculptor sculpts
the head of man:
imposing brow,
cleft chin,
eyes for good
measure.

Why this   1+
with the other?

The stone neck
descending into
crudely chiselled
steps.

The sculptor   1+
has no intent

At the base
of stone steps:
a stone pear.

but to make   1
a stone calculator.

ONE IN, SO MANY OUTS

What types are baby-making nowadays?
The double-wide, the born-again, the set-
in-stone? I wonder about the anxious.

I wonder whether we've gone flaccid
deciding linoleum or artificial oak?

Far too much questioning; far too
few mountings on floors, indiscriminate
of price per square foot.

What types are baby-making nowadays?

CROW'S FEET AXIOM

As dictated by Euclid, he draws
lines to where things end,
embracing coherence through
mismatched points.

Who can draw insecurity,
so tenderly, that women give my
name to children, or lines gracing
the corners of their eyes?

I don't have the patience or palimony,
yet long to hear: "See how she
stares at you with that sidelong glance?
A spitting image of her father —
not the beer-swiller on the couch,
you must understand,
but her spiritual father
and my one true love."

BANGS CHERRY COKE NO RUM

submissive in every way
that doesn't count plus some that

do want excessive stupid drama
like attention and photography

of freaks or pervs or too old or
unattractive people

partying swimming talking
shopping even if

it's bad and illegal I'm generally
like let's graffiti or sketch tattoos of

horrors romance action maybe
indecent chat on here

so honesty crucial
friendship necessary for

Nashville Tennessee to find me
passionate dependable &

drinking virgin
pops again

A IS TO B

A man walks into
your library and, eyeing
the books lining the walls,
asks,
Are you going to read all of those?

:

A man walks into
your bomb shelter and, eyeing
the soup cans lining the walls,
asks,
Are you going to eat all of those?

Given the analogy,
and the number of books you've read,
are we in the midst of an emergency?

SHORT-TERM GOALS ETCHED IN LIQUID GOLD

I want Tom Stoppard
I want to decoupage over something important
I want symmetrical haircuts for everyone but me
for trembling at the lazy expensive fearfulness of my haircut
I want to decoupage decoupage

framed by the beauty of said haircut I want genius grants
(for my intellect only)
I want brains to shun decoration
except paper
and glue and varnish

to drink every word luminous
and the fumes to prompt gold feverish dreams
of new haircuts and methods of decoration
and roads to new men
splashed with glue gold
holding hair unnatural

and do I want
beyond myself
beyond the fashioning of my extremity
beyond the liquid word
to drink of Tom Stoppard
the preserved
lacquered gold?

HERMETIC

The truth is what came after: children
birthing fathers from vacancies in shells.
My father, the engineer, contrived to design
a life by holding half the world at bay.

We miss the promenades and, for that matter,
windows.

Now there's only one bloody footprint
to the bathroom. Where's my landlord
when I need him? All the previous tenants
fell seamlessly into the whole: reductionisms
so dead, and small, and dark, and simple.

I was left in my sister's burial plot,
as to keep the next flood from where
nothing is at all. I, oblivious to halves,
listening to oceans in others' bellies,
knew proximity as mortar and love.

There are some things I won't build you:
pools — how many chemicals would we
need to make them safe for us?

There are some things I can't tell:
murdering my sister by telephone.
With my plan, calls were free
any holiday you paint the shells
of others' offspring, to hide them
from your own.

THE HOME INSPECTION

Before I even step
into this house
let me point out
something about
the foliage.

Those leaves on
that there bush
were new in spring;
given it's late July
I'd say they have
two months tops.

I doubt they're
under warranty.

THREE HOLIEST SITES
OF DULUTH, MINNESOTA

in the backroom
of Johnston's Hardware store
on Fifth and Main
sits a container of thumbtacks
opened in 1987

never will these fasteners
be used again
they are symbols only

like when any crucifix became
the cross

the transitory circle route
of the 124A
from the Sparewoods' suburbs
to Royal Gardens Cemetery
& Golf Course

the closest many get to
daily meditation

& deliverance

this time when you
lace your skates
at Jim's RollerCade
become the music
and the white strobe
light

TAKING MEASURE

Taste a month of men (twenty-eight days, exactly).
Measuring the man-days' worth, each contributes
eighteen decibels of tongue per square inch.

Dividing man-days amongst men (with all uses permissible),
the mean tongue inflates stock prices, whereas the median
devalues ice cream. There is little taste haberdashery or words.

On Sundays men fear the larynx. On Mondays man-tongues
fear the teeth. Male incisors are revered for mathematical
ability (dividing a steak, on average, seventy-one times).

Male tongue temperatures decrease biweekly (correlation
to ice cream indeterminate) bottoming out at languid grey.
The sedentary grey tongue shows predilection to nudity.

The month of men, spoken backwards or forwards, is
the same noise: twenty-eight handsome, bare, mono-
chrome pops, divisible only by themselves.

MORAL

I only want actions with the smallest reactions:
I invite you over for a cigarette
and you die in a car crash.
Sure you were drunk, but smoking killed you,
or I did—
point is we had fun.

LAST EVENINGS: TAIPEI, WILMINGTON

You drank red-stained receipts warning
shopkeepers in unintelligible Mandarin:
insufficient funds. The tea's absence
tasting like exhaust and chrysanthemum.

Streets empty except for the man
who exists as wall-to-wall carpeting
and insists on jostling you between his folds.

In a sly flash of rhetoric, the signs convince
you: you are neon.

This is a ghost town — caught in a tumbleweed
of cement, steel, and glass — with every building
boarded up to you.

By a trick of time zones, your Delaware only
exists twelve hours ahead or past.

Each road in Taiwan dead set on Brandywine
Creek, where the sun rose without morning,
without memory.

COUP D'ÉTAT

". . . we become keenly aware, just as a poem discussing
the Anglo-Zanzibar War can be about mothers, the
inverse is also true. Therefore, what is important in poetry
is not content, but strong internal logic. At its pinnacle,
a poem best resembles a mathematical equation where,
when the reader substitutes himself into the 'mother'
placeholder, subsequent bastard children arise (unless
the author chooses a more direct form of insemination)."
— *Livre sur Livre sur Rien*, Clémence Arbre

the war between Mother and me
is the shortest in recorded history

largely due to my heroics
and because
she was a frail woman
weighing ninety pounds
both soaking wet and holding a
pot roast
as she was apt to do

one day
whilst Mother reclined in the bath
with a chuck steak defrosting
beside her in the warm waters
my ennui sent the tub into a boil
which Mother
ever careless
failed to recognize

"Why is there never a sockeye to be found
soaking next to you . . . never a brisket nor
Cornish game hen stuffed with saffron?"

her insolence demanded action
I was fearful
and honour-bound
to commit

the potato offensive
as guided by God
ricocheted *apples of the earth* off
medicine cabinets
                mirrors
                    vanities
only to strike great vengeance upon
Mother's shrunken palsied head

perhaps there remained
an ounce of stubbornness
for her convulsions held the
gleam of resistance

I pity a man in my position
but reiterate
hands were forced by the divine

it's unclear if she saw the melon's horrific arc
in reverence I shielded my eyes
knowing victory assured

after regaining consciousness
and waving a white washcloth
Mother readily endorsed forms in her
signature squiggle
promising greater cognizance in cooking
and to pay for the damaged produce
from her social security

INVISIBLE FRUIT

We all have our reasons:
my mother was a cat and
Father studied candles
for hours nightly.

Sprinting the fallow orchard,
I say this, all empathy,
you're nutty as a loon.

I wish it was sympathy:
Mom digging wet sand
with her toes, then Dad,
understanding, hair on fire.

Which one is running?
The sentence isn't clear . . .
I always assumed it was you.

ROSE-COLOURED GLASS

Standing tall, respectively resting
on flying buttresses and slots,
the Cathedral of Chartres
and Larry's Gaming and Wedding
Emporium are similarly
successful in what they do.

Most would not trade wads
of cash for their dirty tunic,
however the spires and sculptures
score points.

CENTRAL INTELLIGENCE

we'll grow
as much high-yield profitable information as there has been
in the past ten thousand years
combined

with less bone meal
conserving satellite photography and soil
to improve lives

and do this by selling seeds

it's important
we don't make decisions
stewardship only the president and consumer can exercise
in the absence of choice

fertilize
don't fear

REMOVING CURTAINS

The gauze already seeped morning
yellow. With this bandage removed from
windows, light dripped into rooms.

Tradesmen painted shadows off
walls, lay white tiles over grey.

In this light we danced.

The contractor's utility belt pushed
against my wife's stomach. He built
a smile on her sullen face.

I ran my hand down a shaft of
mop, spun it around, dipping shaggy
hair seductively to the floor. My wife
didn't notice.

> Is the world bleeding (bleeding light)?
> Why remove the bandage?

> If tension exists between light and dark,
> why the sexual interplay between man,
> wife, and tradesman?

INEXORABLE

Ideas falter in the face of it,
it being the most terrible
prudence, and low lying,
and yellow.

A nightingale shivers at its
voice, whereas accountants
frown, resting heads in
soft numbers, soft hands.

It carries the weight of
a medium stone and
your weight half the distance
of any journey.

At the beginning of each year
it soaks in laughter to be hardened
to December's sorrow. It takes
no pleasure in this.

Sitting across from you,
at the dinner table or subway car,
it makes mashed potatoes and newspapers
interesting.

It is embarrassed by averted eyes,
poor posture, how light is lost
on your skin.

It is why the squinter gropes, believing
the sun a candle.

It wants dessert also.

WESTERNS AS AN ALLEGORY OF

For a while they built only false fronts,
both beautiful and troublesome,
for when I threw a man through
their ornately framed windows
never was there a question of pursuit.

Instead the assailed
leisurely chews sugar glass,
rearranging a bolo tie
neatly around his neck.

The cameraman,
as bored as I,
passes me a cigarillo.

Distracted by smoke-rings,
to be CGed in later,
I miss the man make a break
for an old wagon that,
not extending far enough
into the third dimension,
tips like a gambler
deep in winnings and bourbon.

I would continue the chase,
but the scriptwriter thinks audiences
will grasp his point.

WHEN HE DID WHAT HE DID

Where were the alarms? Was everything
slipshod? No need for authorities to douse
fires, sweep floors, start anew?

He was an abolitionist: that is to say against
working, against numbers nine through
five, against so many credits to make
Sunday, two more than you have
but we'll spot you, with juice.

When He Did What He Did it wasn't an act,
not a pantomime pre-tank, nor naked
for no fur, no liberal icecap jamboree.

The What He Did was coordinated,
had a t-shirt, a slogan: I have a slogan, ask.
When the caffeinated, dreary, work-
a-days inquired, the What He Did was not
apparent.

But it stared us in the face: ol' two eyes.
The What He Did, the fire five finger life
discount, the arm abandonment, that limbless
slap, infuriated us into complacency.

We didn't know, in our agitated peace, how much
the What He Did had no effect on us,
and as such ruled us completely.

I often don't wonder if that was his plan all along,
as I fail to build smoke detectors for treason.

THE TWO GRANDFATHERS

Darryl and Dean Walker were identical twins
everyone could tell apart.
Dean's appendectomy scar was a dead
giveaway, though both brothers' tendency to remain
clothed in public, at least while sober,
rendered this moot.

Less obvious was the half-grin Darryl wore,
as if choking down a joke. There was also
Dean's missing arm.

Later, when asked to recall the moment
things went wrong, they responded in unison,
"December 5, 1933."

Prior to this, the depression was kind.
Most had no money for staples, but
whisky sales remained brisk; the amber elixir cured all
be it hunger or joblessness.

Before the Ontario Prohibition,
in 1916, the brothers sold apples and cider vinegar
for change, to buy imported Toledo whisky
for dollars. Despite the lopsided math, it was
a pleasant enough equation.

As supplies of whisky dwindled, with society's noble
experiment, prices rose and quality fell. The brothers
found themselves forced into clandestine midnight
rendezvous, all for glasses of watered-down gold.

Robbed of his spirit, Darryl's smirk fell fowl.
After weeks of drying out, Dean's languid
mind formed an idea that, lonely in its shell, escaped
quickly and unimpeded:

                           to become bootleggers.

THE SHORT FATHER

I'm ornately bookended by the remarkable,
leaving me an unread entertainment, solely for myself.

On one side: snake-oil salesman and industrious,
if simple-minded, drunks. The other side: the future.

THE PRESENT

Why do we do what we do? I frivolously dress necessity to
make it appear as choice: a charming brownstone; penny
loafers; filet mignon.

I inherit a set of genes and drunken fortune that precludes
all work. I collect pinball machines, travelling the Eastern
Seaboard in search of a Williams 1951, nickel-play
Hayburners, or 1964 Grand Slam Pitch & Bat.

There is no logic in this. I'm simply witnessing the playing
out of events: a steel ball shot forth, colliding with whatever
targets are set before it.

I used to believe, in studying the past, you could project
understanding through the future's linear flow. I charted
family trees with broken and unknown limbs. I flunked
HMB201: Introduction to Genes, Genetics, and Biotechnology.

But the past inevitably descends into myth.
Stories of grandparents become fables.
Tumble back far enough (England? Jakarta? Jerusalem?)
and history becomes a blank wall to graffiti what you will.

bestow gratuitously that which ought to be given
the thing or animal referred to bound in duty to be bestowed
gratuitously to an individual human or divine being looked fixedly at
assume to what produces effect
to have being or draw near to be clear and calm
and grasp an item held as property
fairly correct the characteristic of a particular person having the
    qualities of a man
or superhumanly beautiful or intelligent person or thing that exists
with things done to make ready
bring to entirety
for use
services for a design of effecting something
take upon oneself

ORANGE

Accused of being orange
I never exhaled again, becoming
the dead-end filter to my cigarette.

Black from smoke, I was still
orange. Work was blown. Poverty
became proof of orange.

A pyramid scheme, the key
to green was people below, but
gravity lifted everything

away, except smoke
settling in soles of my dingy,
orange shoes.

TWO PIECES OF "WHY"

1)

I didn't realize that the French word *inflammable*
means *flammable* in English.

11)

There are two shelves above the bar. We created
a new shot by randomly mixing bottle eleven
on the bottom with bottle six on top:
sambuca and scotch.

"What will we call it?"
"Fuck Yer Face."

They stained the deck knowing
they would do it again in four
short years, and again four years

later. Four years after that they
would hire someone to do it, or
their kids would, or they'd be

dead. The way the water beads
off the deck now looks like tears.
Don't get sentimental you stupid

STAINED CEDAR

Tried to end world hunger
by feeding myself

TWO HEIRLOOM TOMATOES

We went on like nothing happened,
emptying gills into neighbours' pockets,
who in turn slapped us while reciting

wet alphabets. It wasn't entirely
informative (we couldn't breathe).
I wanted new airy letters

inspiring words outside
my weary lexicon. I wanted
sounds to approximate

GOLDFISH TEARS

CARAVAGGIO OUT OF ORDER

Opportunity for fingers thrust
in burnt umber pigments.
1602 paints narratives like 1962 paints
paint, pencil scraps, typewriter keys
(doubting Thomas muted).

Nothing surrounds the man
but what the man sees in himself.

The painting presents itself
for you are its completion.

Glass hinting at an outside world.
Here: the cherries ripe. The rose?
Perhaps too much so. The boy?
The lizard doesn't seem to mind.

Eight years later, a greater acknowledgment
of further rot.

Light out of grasp, earthly
pearls discarded, yet in reach
of arms, not your own but Mary's from the Pieta:
penitent for what hands couldn't do.

A ram stretches its neck in lieu of the boy's.

Saint Jerome knows Latin's a dead language.

Cupid, shown asleep earlier, has his job
usurped by Saint Ursula's pagan suitor:
spurting blood attests true love.

SUN BLOCK DAYS

Fear was young in Nebraska
when days fell from crescent moons.
Mornings: seawater on skin
to prevent the pull.

Aunt Nebraska waned
fields, husks to valuable dirt,
whilst succumbing to corn cough.

Danger, born luxurious, to a family
of astronomers, slept
well into the risen third moon,
when mothers waxed breakfast.

Incongruous eggs formed
narratives, climaxing
to waves of bat sonar.

Indifference held till nothing,
at confused midnight,
pierced the SPF leaves.

POETRY TODAY

A man comes to a reading to get a book of poetry signed.
This volume is of particular interest to the man because
he has read and enjoyed its copyright page immensely;
a smile is brought to lips every time he sees the words
"first edition" in fine print. As the author scrawls his
name across the front free endpaper, the man is already
imagining the fantastical bids it will receive when listed
on the internet. Yes, the man enjoys poetry very much.

LACHRYMOSE

Children's faulty counting:
no conception of their
parents' deception by geothermic
magma convection posters
devised by those who question
no deeper than distances
measured in feet.

They came in white coats,
placing posters on my window,
followed by school groups
and lonely men posing as
the Renaissance.

Whether the geyser came
or not, it can't help but be
a disappointment.

REGISTRY

(Mr. Gray, 1972)

As the wedding date draws near,
so too the worry grows at my lack of gift.

Remembering I'm the groom,
search for fidelity on the gift registry
to no avail, only flatware remains.

(Mrs. Gray, 2003)

My joy resides in two beautiful children,
a punch bowl, and set of sterling silver.

Watching him carefully polish the spoons,
I know he's come to realize the bowl
and the children aren't his.

THE FINITE STRETCHED EAR

Tuesday, one hundred and thirty-six
thousand news stories coughed.

A Liberian diplomat downed
democracy in a Manhattan.

A famous pair of underwear mistakenly
revealed their owner while exiting a cab.

Yet
no one scooped the (inauspicious?)
bronchitis drowning of Raymond LeRue.

And
Sally Danforth first tasted air
to little fanfare.

Gasps remain inaudible behind
removed guilt, small pleasures.

WAYS TO FRAME AN ARGUMENT

I went to the gallery and found my
neighbour, nailed to the wall, chastising
other paintings for disregard to
geometry.

The imprudence of the non-triangle;
what's the point if not three?

EACH FRUIT CONTAINS ITS SEED

The town was designed thoughtfully
prior to the memory of those you remember;
barbershop, pharmacy, grocery
aligned in pleasing rows
too straight to be coincidental.

Whereas histories exist of our forefathers,
nothing shall be written on us.
We await the town showing our chosen path.
When Luke, the shopkeeper, passed
I began arranging apples in requisite pyramids.

There is talk of erecting a bowling alley,
but if such a thing were warranted,
surely it would be here already.

ENDING THE MIGRATION

The play elaborately spanned two continents,
tipping the balance of North and South on its side.
Half the children dressed in: khakis, fatigues, pith hats.
The others: tarred, attached to pulleys, brightly feathered.

At a preordained moment the winged-ones ascend,
yanked by ropes (to great applause),
then swung at by lassoes or targeted
by volleys of tranquilizer darts.

Poor Gertrude hit so many times her
strident snores rained spittle upon the audience.

We watched, implicitly cheering, by looking
into the depths of our popcorn bags.

ANSWER KEY

grapefruit juice: a sign
empty dustpans: a symptom
children crossing the road: a sign
overturned chairs: a sign
winter: a symptom
security cameras at Laundromats: a sign and a symptom
tennis shoes over a telephone wire: a sign
the first Beaujolais of the season: a sign
colour television: a sign then a symptom
foreign policy: a symptom

THE DUNDREARY-ARTS

I collect parables for those proud to kneel
At the overwhelming and incomprehensible.

There's a cupboard of decorative plates, obscured
With sustenance and pleasure: President Lincoln
Freeing lima beans; an eagle and mashed potatoes.

Every note dropped from national anthems slumbers
In gilt-framed, matted prints of smallpox victims:
Little Donavon Vickers, an unwanted piccolo solo,
Can't breathe a note. Honest Abe's here again.

I've washed the floor in penitence for the frightful
Size of whales, aghast at the sacrilege of dust.

To be clean one must: be sanitized of floor; accept
History; care for sick melodies; honour foodstuffs;
Understand sea life as symbols of unbridled gluttony.

Do you not believe in Lincoln? We have his holy hat.
What of smallpox? We've not the dodo, but he sung.
One rests on the righteous who, clean from floor upwards,
Carries the grace of winged beasts on mind and plate.

In days' grace form your cast from a rosary of peas,
For night chides, "Sic semper tyrannis!" to life's theatre.
If the crowd cheers you're on the wrong side of infamy.
Mass panic, the desired response, rests you in time.

The blood voices and night stage are all encased in art.
This is why we have walls, to hold yesterday's creditors.

What is the parable of the whale? He floats wall-less,
Without history, secure in his girth like a slumbering god.
Awake: we have a silver dollar with your name.

Acknowledgements

Thanks to the editors at *Grain* and *West Wind Review*,
where earlier versions of these poems previously appeared.